VIGO COUNTY PUBLIC LIBRARY
TERRE HAUTE, INDIANA

W9-ANF-170

Computers to Tablets

WITHDRAWN

Then to Now Tech

By Jennifer Colby

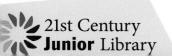

21st Century
Junior Library

CHERRY LAKE
Publishing

Published in the United States of America by
Cherry Lake Publishing
Ann Arbor, Michigan
www.cherrylakepublishing.com

Content Adviser: Adam Fulton Johnson, PhD History of Science and Technology, University of Michigan
Reading Adviser: Marla Conn, MS, Ed., Literacy specialist, Read-Ability, Inc.

Photo Credits: ©Alena Kravchenko/Shutterstock.com, Cover, 1 [left]; ©A3pfamily/Shutterstock.com, Cover, 2 [right];
©De Agostini Picture Library/agefotostock.com, 4; ©INTERFOTO/alamy.com, 6; ©Everett Historical/Shutterstock.com, 8;
U.S. Census Bureau, 10; ©MIND AND I/Shutterstock.com, 12; ©dean bertoncelj/Shutterstock.com, 14; ©travelview/iStock.com, 16;
©Anton_Ivanov/Shutterstock.com, 18; ©Syda Productions/Shutterstock.com, 20

Copyright © 2020 by Cherry Lake Publishing
All rights reserved. No part of this book may be reproduced or utilized in any
form or by any means without written permission from the publisher.

Library of Congress Cataloging-in-Publication Data
Names: Colby, Jennifer, 1971- author.
Title: Computers to tablets / Jennifer Colby.
Description: Ann Arbor : Cherry Lake Publishing, [2019] | Series: Then to now tech |
    Includes bibliographical references and index.
Identifiers: LCCN 2019004223| ISBN 9781534147287 (hardcover) | ISBN
    9781534148710 (pdf) | ISBN 9781534150140 (pbk.) | ISBN 9781534151574
    (hosted ebook)
Subjects: LCSH: Electronic digital computers–History–Juvenile literature.
Classification: LCC QA76.23 .C643 2019 | DDC 004–dc23
LC record available at https://lccn.loc.gov/2019004223

Cherry Lake Publishing would like to acknowledge the work of the Partnership for 21st Century Skills.
Please visit *www.p21.org* for more information.

Printed in the United States of America
Corporate Graphics

CONTENTS

Does this look like a computer to you? Babbage's Analytical Engine is considered one of the first designs of a modern computer.

The First Computer

Englishman Charles Babbage imagined the first computer in the 1830s. Its basic parts are in the computers of today: a **central processing unit** and **memory**. But he never built the entire machine in his lifetime. It existed only on paper.

The German Z3 was the first electronic computer.

Demands of War

The first working electronic computers were built in the mid-20th century. There was a great need to **process** information quickly during World War II. Scientists and mathematicians in Germany, England, and the United States created the machines to do so.

These early computers were all based on a system of rules to compute data

The American ENIAC computer was 150 feet (45.7 meters) wide!

developed by British mathematician Alan Turing. German engineer Konrad Zuse built the Z3 in 1941. It was the world's first **programmable** digital computer. Britain's Colossus was a set of code-breaking computers completed in 1944. The United States' ENIAC was completed in 1945. It could process 5,000 addition problems in one second!

Look!

What were other early computers? Ask an adult to help you search the internet to find some.

Computers filled entire rooms!

Computermania!

In 1946, the inventors of the ENIAC began work on a computer for the U.S. Census Bureau. The census is an official count of people in the United States. The new UNIVAC was one of the first **commercial** computers.

Computers need specific instructions called programs. Computer code is the line-by-line set of instructions that tells a computer what to do. In 1953, Grace Hopper created the first programming language called COBOL.

Lines of code are created by a **programmer**.

New technology resulted in new kinds of computers. The first computer with a **graphical user interface** was invented in 1963. This type of computer is what most people use today. It allows you to operate a computer without having to enter computer coding instructions.

The creation of personal computers made it possible for many people to own a computer.

In 1976, Steve Jobs and Steve Wozniak created the Apple I. This first Apple computer sold for $666.66. It consisted of only one **circuit board**. Users had to provide their own case, keyboard, and monitor.

Make a Guess!

About 200 Apple I units were made. How many do you think still exist? How much do you think they are worth today? Ask an adult to help you find out.

The internet grew from a network of connected colleges.

Information in Our Hands

All these computers needed to connect with each other. A network of phone lines allowed computers at major U.S. universities to share information with each other. It was called ARPANET. It became the internet.

Soon everyone wanted to share information around the world. Tim Berners-Lee invented the concept of the World Wide Web in 1989. The web is a digital space with

Early tablet computers used a **stylus**.

"pages" of information connected to each other over the internet. We call these pages **websites**.

Over time, devices became smaller and smaller. The idea of tablet computers grew from 1960s science-fiction movies and books. But it wasn't until the 1990s and 2000s that these early computing devices became common.

Think!

How can you find websites? Ask an adult to help you search the internet to find information about a topic from multiple websites.

Tablet computers are now in many schools and homes.

Many people use tablet devices today. They are **portable** and easy to use. What will future tablets look like? Developers are creating new tablet designs. Some are flexible like paper. And some are made with see-through glass!

Ask Questions!

Take a poll. Who uses tablets more, adults or children? Ask an adult to help you.

GLOSSARY

central processing unit (SEN-truhl PRAH-ses-ing YOO-nit) the part of a computer system that performs the computer's main functions and controls the other parts of the system; also referred to as CPU

circuit board (SUR-kit BORD) a sheet of material with many electrical connections

commercial (kuh-MUR-shuhl) for sale

graphical user interface (GRAF-ih-kuhl YOOZ-ur IN-tur-fase) a program that allows a person to work easily with a computer by using icons and other elements on the screen; also referred to as GUI

memory (MEM-uh-ree) capacity for storing information

portable (POR-tuh-buhl) easy to carry or move around

process (PRAH-ses) to take in and use

programmable (proh-GRAM-uh-buhl) able to be told what to do

programmer (PROH-gram-er) a person who creates computer programs

stylus (STYE-luhs) a small tool that is used to write or touch buttons on a computer

websites (WEB-sites) places or pages on the World Wide Web that contain information about a topic and are usually linked to other web pages by hyperlinks

FIND OUT MORE

BOOKS

Kamar, Haq. *The Evolution of Computer Technology*. New York, NY: Rosen Publishing, 2018.

Oachs, Emily Rose. *The Personal Computer*. Minnetonka, MN: Bellwether Media, 2019.

WEBSITES

DK Find Out!—First Computers
https://www.dkfindout.com/us/science/amazing-inventions/first-computers
Find out more about the first computer and the first home computer, and see what they looked like.

Wonderopolis—When Is Technology Old?
https://wonderopolis.org/wonder/when-is-technology-old
Find out why new technology replaces old technology and try some activities.

INDEX

ABOUT THE AUTHOR

Jennifer Colby is a school librarian in Ann Arbor, Michigan. She loves reading, traveling, and going to museums to learn about new things.